AUTHOR	
TITLE	
DATE DUE	BORROWER'S NAME

BOOKFRIENDS INTERNATIONAL

A donation to your School / Library

THE SCHOOL THE AZTEC EAGLES BUILT

A TRIBUTE TO MEXICO'S WORLD WAR II AIR FIGHTERS

In memory of Ángel Bocanegra del Castillo, schoolteacher and valiant Aztec Eagle soldier who held up high the flag of Mexico and gave his village a school. Your students and teachers at Escuela Squadron 201 in Tepoztlán will always remember you and the men of the 201st Mexican Fighter Squadron.

Mexican government officials with Air Fighter Squadron 201 pilots and ground crew members

THE SCHOOL THE AZTEC EAGLES BUILT

A TRIBUTE TO MEXICO'S WORLD WAR II AIR FIGHTERS

by Dorinda Makanaōnalani Nicholson

Lee & Low Books Inc.
New York

MEXICO AND THE UNITED STATES JOIN FORCES

Mexico and the United States were not always allies. At one time the two countries were enemies fighting battles over the northern territories of Mexico and its border with the United States. By the 1830s there were four times more US settlers living in the Mexican province of Tejas (Texas) than Mexican-born settlers. At first the Texans, as settlers living in that region were called, agreed to obey Mexican laws, but eventually cultural and political differences among the distinct groups led to many disputes and uprisings. The conflicts came to a head when Mexico instituted a new government that outlawed certain rights and upheld the abolishment of slavery. The Texans objected to absolute Mexican rule and, in 1835, declared their independence from Mexico.

Mexico fought hard to keep Tejas; but after the Battle of San Jacinto in April 1836, in which a great number of Mexican soldiers were killed or taken prisoner, Texan troops captured Mexican president Antonio López de Santa Anna. He was then forced to sign a treaty giving Tejas its independence. Mexico's congress refused to ratify the treaty and continued to claim Tejas as part of Mexico.

The fighting over the new Republic of Tejas continued unofficially for ten more years. At the same time, the United States was determined to expand its territories and offered to annex the Republic of Tejas. In 1845, the people of Tejas agreed to become the twenty-eighth US state: Texas. Now the struggle over the border became a war between the United States and Mexico.

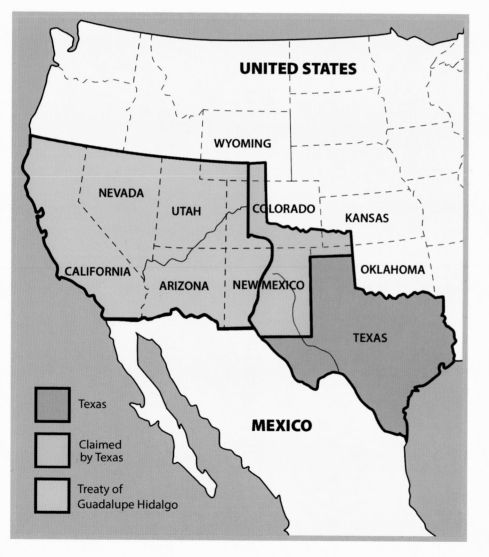

UNITED STATES

WYOMING

NEVADA

UTAH

COLORADO

KANSAS

CALIFORNIA

ARIZONA

NEW MEXICO

OKLAHOMA

TEXAS

MEXICO

- Texas
- Claimed by Texas
- Treaty of Guadalupe Hidalgo

Mexican president Antonio López de Santa Anna

The conflict, known as the US-Mexican War, lasted from 1846 until 1848. In the end, Mexico lost Texas and the land that became California, Nevada, Utah, Arizona, New Mexico, and parts of Colorado and Wyoming in the Treaty of Guadalupe Hidalgo. It is also estimated that approximately twenty-five thousand Mexican soldiers were killed or wounded. The war was a bitter defeat for Mexico, and relations between Mexico and the United States remained tense for almost one hundred years.

Reconciliation between the two countries began during the 1930s with the United States government's Good Neighbor policy toward Latin American countries and was further solidified in the midst of World War II. In May 1942, German U-boats torpedoed two unarmed Mexican oil tankers. Mexico protested the submarine attacks, but Germany ignored the protest. Mexico then declared war on the Axis powers—Germany, Italy, and Japan—and entered World War II on the side of the Allied powers.

United States president Franklin D. Roosevelt and Mexican president Manuel Ávila Camacho met to discuss how their countries could work together in the war effort. One eventual result was the formation of the Mexican Expeditionary Air Force. Its flight operations unit was Air Fighter Squadron 201—also known as the Aztec Eagles.

Mexico and the United States were now allies united against common enemies.

Poster showing Mexican sombrero and Uncle Sam–style top hat united to fight in World War II

ÁNGEL BOCANEGRA
TEPOZTLÁN, MORELOS, MEXICO

Ángel Bocanegra del Castillo was born in Tepoztlán, Morelos, in 1918. The village of Tepoztlán sprawls below an ancient Aztec pyramid that appears to stand guard over the valley below. In the town center the cobblestone marketplace is typically crowded with eager vendors. Nearby, church bells chime away the hours.

Ángel's father, a high-ranking soldier during the Mexican Revolution, earned the rank of division general. He believed military service was an important civic duty, and he expected Ángel to follow in his footsteps by attending military school and then joining the army. But when Ángel was eighteen, he decided to become a teacher instead. He loved to craft words into poetry and song lyrics, and to make people laugh with prepared or impromptu speeches. Ángel also decided to marry Laura Quiroz Concha. Laura dreamed of becoming a teacher too. They planned to teach together in their village.

Tepoztlán's elementary school had two small classrooms. Only the third-grade and sixth-grade students fit into the tiny rooms. Students in the other grades crowded into the nearby convent. When the convent space filled up, students had no choice but to sit outdoors.

Ángel taught his fourth graders in a garden under the shade of wide-spreading fruit trees. Laura took her little first graders to a grassy slope so they could sit on an angle and see her better. Other teachers used the porches of nearby homes as classrooms. The trees and porches provided partial protection from the brutally hot sun, but when it rained, school had to be canceled. Ángel and Laura wished their village had a school big enough to fit all the students.

After a few years, Ángel and Laura were the proud parents of a little girl. Ángel's father pleaded with him to join the military. If Ángel became a soldier, he would earn more money and be better able to provide for his family. Ángel eventually followed his father's advice. He left his teaching position and enlisted in the Mexican army.

Ángel Bocanegra; dedication written to his wife, Laura, at the bottom right

WORLD WAR II COMES TO NORTH AMERICA
1941–1942

On December 7, 1941, Japanese planes bombed Pearl Harbor, Hawaii. The surprise attack forced the United States into World War II against the Axis powers. The United States joined with the Allied powers to fight against these nations in Europe and the Pacific.

Even though Mexico had no plans to participate in direct warfare, the country pledged support and aid to the United States. Mexican ships began delivering valuable crude oil and other much-needed war materials to the United States. Mexico also closed its ports to German ships. These actions made Mexico a target for German submarine attacks.

On May 13, 1942, a German U-boat prowling the waters off the coast of Florida torpedoed an unarmed Mexican oil tanker, the *Potrero del Llano*, bound for the United States. Thirteen crew members were killed. The Mexican government filed an official protest with the German government. Instead of acknowledging or giving compensation for the loss, Germany responded on May 22 with a U-boat attack on a second Mexican oil tanker, this time killing eight of the crew. Mexico was left with little choice but to declare war on the Axis nations, which the country did on May 28.

The United States quickly shipped airplanes to Mexico so the country could patrol and protect its coastline. But with only a small, underfunded peacetime army, Mexico was unable to participate more actively in the war. In fact, in the country's history, Mexico had never sent armed forces to fight in a foreign country.

Oil tanker Potrero del Llano *burning after being torpedoed by a German U-boat off the coast of Florida*

MEXICO BREAKS TRADITION
1943–1944

The April 20, 1943, visit of President Roosevelt to Monterrey, Mexico, was a military secret until just a few hours before the president's train pulled into the railroad station. On arrival, Roosevelt was given a twenty-one-gun salute, and a military band played the national anthems of both the United States and Mexico.

In a radio broadcast that evening, President Ávila Camacho ended his speech by saying, "I repeat to you, Mr. President, together with the sentiments of solidarity of my country and our wish for the success of our common cause, the desire that the relations between Mexico and the United States of America may develop—always—along the channels of mutual esteem and unceasing devotion to liberty."

Mexican president Manuel Ávila Camacho (left) and United States president Franklin D. Roosevelt arrive in Monterrey, Mexico, in an open car

Thousands of Mexican laborers standing in line to sign up for the Bracero Program

The meeting in Monterrey marked the first of several collaborative summits between the two presidents. They initiated the Bracero Program, an agreement that allowed Mexicans to enter the United States on temporary work permits. From 1943 to 1945, more than one hundred thousand *braceros*, or laborers, worked on farms and railroads, helping to alleviate the labor shortage caused when American soldiers were sent to Europe and Asia to fight. The Mexican government saw the Bracero Program as one way to contribute to the war effort.

After some initial reluctance, President Ávila Camacho also decided to break tradition and send Mexican troops to fight overseas. A former general, he knew he could not ready a full-scale army in time, but he could send pilots from his air force along with support staff. With the approval of the Mexican Senate and the people of the country, Ávila Camacho arranged to send one air force squadron under Mexican command to fight in the war. President Roosevelt in turn agreed to accept the squadron for training in the United States to prepare the men for duty in the Pacific.

About thirty of Mexico's top-notch pilots, selected from among the best air specialists in the country, were chosen for the training group. Approximately two hundred sixty additional men were also handpicked to support the pilots and maintain the aircraft by repairing, arming, and refueling the planes. Among the support team was a former teacher, now ground crew member: Sergeant Ángel Bocanegra.

A TEACHER'S REQUEST
JULY 20, 1944

The newly formed elite Mexican squadron was eager to start combat training. On July 20, 1944, President Ávila Camacho arrived at Balbuena Military Camp to bid the soldiers farewell before they left for the United States. The uniformed men, standing in parade formation, were proud to pass in review before the president. The march began: pilots first, then the support team. Near the rear, Sergeant Bocanegra—chin up, chest out, arms at his sides—stepped in cadence with the other soldiers.

President Ávila Camacho addressed the men standing at attention before him. He thanked them for their service and asked if anyone had a last-minute or special request before he left.

After a moment of silence, a soldier in the rear stepped forward and saluted.

"Mi presidente," he said. "I am Ángel Bocanegra del Castillo, and, sir, I request that a school be built in my hometown of Tepoztlán, Morelos."

Mexican president Ávila Camacho salutes his troops as they prepare to leave for the United States

President Ávila Camacho, surprised by the unusual request and impressed by Ángel's courage, agreed to have the school built.

Four days later, on July 24, the men of the training group, heavily loaded with gear, scrambled onto train cars in Mexico City. Government officials and crowds of people came to send off the first military unit in history to leave Mexico on a fighting mission.

As the train pulled away from the station, Ángel leaned out a window to say good-bye to his family one last time. Then, settling back in his seat, Ángel smiled, thinking about the new school that would be built in his village.

Families and friends gather to send off the Mexican squadron for training in the United States

POCATELLO AIR FORCE BASE, IDAHO, USA
LATE JULY–NOVEMBER 27, 1944

After crossing into the United States at Laredo, Texas, the group continued to Randolph Field in San Antonio for their specialized base-training assignments. The ground crew was sent on to Pocatello Air Force Base in Idaho. The high, jagged mountains surrounding the base reminded Ángel of the pointed peaks overlooking Tepoztlán.

When he wasn't training, Ángel loved to laugh, tease, and talk with the other ground crew members. Like Ángel, his friend Lieutenant Héctor Espinosa Galván was married and had children. The two talked about how they missed their families and wished they could be home to celebrate Mexico's Independence Day on September 16. Ángel was encouraged by Lieutenant Espinosa Galván and other crew members to deliver an Independence Day speech to the homesick soldiers. Later, in a letter to his family, Ángel wrote that he was honored to speak to the men on the day when Mexicans all over the world celebrated their country's independence from Spain.

In October the pilots joined the ground crew at Pocatello, and the men quickly got to work. The pilots would be flying P-47 Thunderbolt fighter

P-47 Thunderbolt fighter airplane

airplanes, which the mechanics nicknamed Peh-Cuas, short for P-47 in Spanish. The Peh-Cuas were huge and heavy, weighing more than 7 tons (6.35 metric tons) each. They were also powerful and fast. Each plane carried eight 0.50-inch (12.7-millimeter) caliber machine guns and one or two 1,000-pound (454-kilogram) bombs. The pilots agreed the Peh-Cuas were not easy to fly, but they considered them to be great fighter planes.

Ten or eleven ground crew soldiers were assigned to each pilot to arm, supply, inspect, and service his airplane. The support crew was critical to the pilot's success and safety. The teamwork required to maintain the planes fostered a deep bond among the men. The soldiers also found it comforting to speak Spanish among themselves, especially when they teased one another.

Lieutenant Héctor Espinosa Galván

Mexican pilots learning English

Good soldier

THE WAC

WOMEN'S ARMY CORPS

Apply at U.S. Army Recruiting Station or ask your local Postmaster

More than 150,000 women served in the Women's Army Corps (WAC) during World War II; in 1978, the WAC was disbanded, and female and male army units were combined

Part of the training the Mexican pilots received involved learning to speak and read English. It was crucial that the pilots be able to communicate effectively with the US control towers and American pilots before their first flight mission. Women from a unit of the Women's Army Corps (WAC) stationed at Pocatello were recruited to help the Mexican pilots learn English.

An early start to winter made training difficult. The Mexicans were not accustomed to Idaho's bone-chilling, below-zero temperatures, and the cold, harsh weather made servicing the planes almost impossible. Flights were frequently canceled due to low visibility and icy runways. Among Ángel's duties was driving people as well as transporting parts and supplies around the base. Ángel always had a smile, and he kept his passengers entertained with stories while driving them quickly to their destinations in the bitter cold.

To avoid additional delays in their training, the group's commander, Colonel Antonio Cárdenas Rodríguez, requested that his men be moved to a warmer climate. On November 27, the training group headed south to hot, dry Greenville, Texas.

Colonel Antonio Cárdenas Rodríguez

Squadron members braving the snow and bitter-cold winter weather in Idaho

GREENVILLE, TEXAS, USA
LATE NOVEMBER 1944–MID MARCH 1945

As the train entered Greenville, Ángel was excited to be in Texas, and closer to Mexico. He and many of the other soldiers hoped to find some Mexican food in the town's restaurants. Instead they encountered discrimination from the local residents. Restaurants refused to serve the men. Signs such as "No Spanish or Mexicans" appeared in shop windows. And pilots' wives who had traveled to the training base with their husbands could not find off-base housing because no one would rent to them.

Signs such as this appeared outside restaurants throughout Texas

The military base officers at Majors Field, where the training group was stationed, appealed to Greenville's officials to treat their Mexican allies with courtesy. The officials agreed. Some of the racist signs came down, rental apartments were found, and interactions between the Mexican soldiers and the townspeople improved.

The pilots trained intensively in the P-47s. The dangerous program included ground attack, air combat, acrobatics, instrument flying and navigation, and high-altitude flight. At the end of December 1944, the Mexican Senate granted President Ávila Camacho official authority to send the soldiers overseas. The training group was then redesignated the Fuerza Aérea Expedicionaria Mexicana (FAEM)—Mexican Expeditionary Air Force—and its flight operations unit was designated Escuadrón Aéreo de Pelea 201—Air Fighter Squadron 201.

On February 22, 1945, the FAEM graduated and was declared ready for combat. Squadron 201's assignment was to help the United States liberate the Philippines from the Japanese. The squadron headed west to California on March 18 to start its journey to the Pacific.

During their training the members of Squadron 201 had come to call themselves the Águilas Aztecas, the Aztec Eagles. The name linked the image of Aztec warriors with the symbolism of the eagle, known for its strength and powerful, swift attacks. It was a fitting description of the squadron and its forthcoming mission.

Squadron 201 ready for combat after February 22, 1945, graduation; inset: Águilas Aztecas (Aztec Eagles) emblem

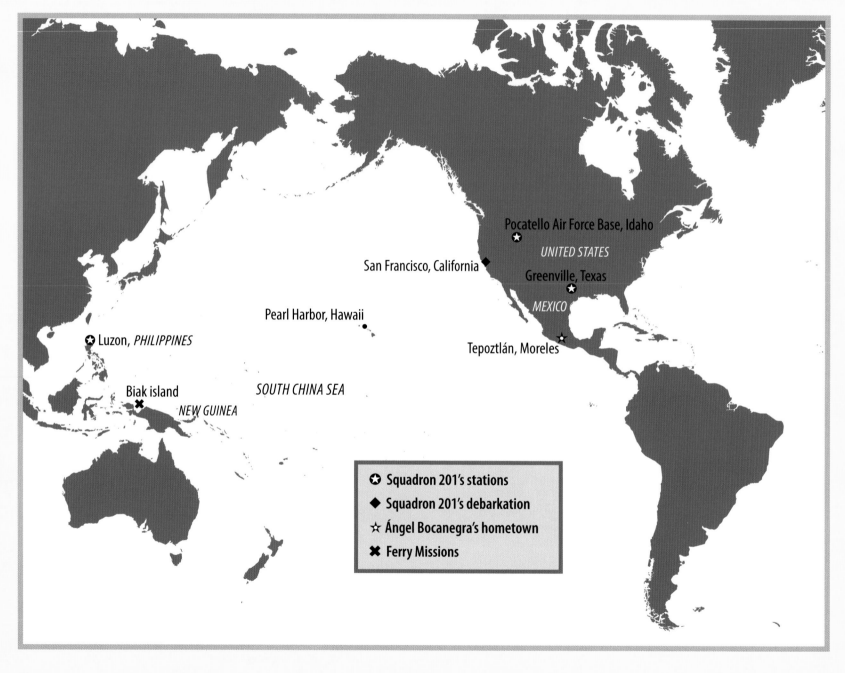

Pocatello Air Force Base, Idaho

UNITED STATES

San Francisco, California

Greenville, Texas

MEXICO

Pearl Harbor, Hawaii

Luzon, *PHILIPPINES*

Tepoztlán, Moreles

Biak island

NEW GUINEA

SOUTH CHINA SEA

✪ Squadron 201's stations
◆ Squadron 201's debarkation
☆ Ángel Bocanegra's hometown
✖ Ferry Missions

The Aztec Eagles traveled by train to San Francisco, where on March 27 they boarded the USS *Fairisle* troop ship and joined fifteen hundred US servicemen. They were bound for warfare in the Philippines.

Cranes loaded the food and equipment needed for the almost 7,000-mile (11,265-kilometer) voyage. Ángel wondered how the small ship would hold all the supplies.

After all their training, Mexican pilots anxiously await their first combat missions

But the men managed to cram the cargo into every available space atop the ship's steel-gray deck.

Below the deck it was just as crowded. As the squadron descended the stairways in the midsection of the boat, they found the cramped area where the hundreds of men would bunk together. Army gear, bedding, and bulging backpacks were piled high against the walls and jammed into corners.

Once the *Fairisle* was fully loaded and the anchor cranked up, the ship passed under the Golden Gate Bridge. As they moved into the open sea, the soldiers realized the dangers of their mission. They were now in enemy waters!

To avoid being torpedoed by enemy submarines, the USS *Fairisle* zigzagged across the Pacific Ocean, adding miles to the journey. The first few days at sea, the water was relatively calm. Then the ocean became rough and choppy. Anything that was not tied down rolled around as the ship rocked back and forth. Some of the men were seasick, and the screaming sirens that signaled emergency training drills made the men nervous.

During the day the soldiers exercised to keep their muscles strong. It was not easy to jog over the equipment and personal belongings piled everywhere, so most of the time the men just ran in place. Duffel bags stuffed with anything heavy were used as weights. At night, the men passed the time playing games and cards, and some of the squadron members, including Sergeant Neftalí González Corona, played Mexican melodies on their guitars. "The journey was made bearable by the happy spirit of the squadron," one soldier wrote.

Sergeant Neftalí González Corona entertaining soldiers during the trip across the Pacific on the USS Fairisle

Construction of a new school in Tepoztlán; President Ávila Camacho did not forget his promise to Ángel Bocanegra

As the *Fairisle* neared the Philippines, Squadron 201 was placed under the command of US general Douglas MacArthur, supreme Allied commander of the Southwest Pacific Area. General MacArthur was pleased to have the squadron join his forces, and President Ávila Camacho was proud to have his soldiers led by the famous general.

President Ávila Camacho was also reminded of his promise to Sergeant Ángel Bocanegra. The president sent a construction crew to Tepoztlán. There they found the tiny school in the hilltops. The president ordered that construction of the new school begin right away so the building would be completed by the time Squadron 201 returned home from the war.

Front entrance of the school under construction

PORAC AIRFIELD, PHILIPPINES
MAY 1–JUNE 1945

The *Fairisle* slid into Manila Bay on May 1, 1945, after five weeks at sea. Well wishes and good-byes were exchanged between the squadron members and their US troop ship buddies who were headed off to other stations.

The Aztec Eagles traveled by train to their military base, Porac, a small airfield on the island of Luzon in the Philippines not far from the larger Clark Air Base. The Porac airfield had a single dirt runway that the Aztec Eagles shared with their new partners, the 58th Fighter Group of the US Fifth Air Force.

The 58th Fighter Group trained the Mexican pilots, who were now under the command of Captain Radamés Gaxiola Andrade. Advanced combat training began immediately to ready the Aztec Eagles for flying and bombing missions. They were outfitted with used P-47 Thunderbolts, the same type of Peh-Cuas they had trained with in Idaho.

Conchita Carmelo, daughter of Mexico's consul to the Philippines, greeting Mexican pilots when they arrive in Luzon

At first, inclusion of Squadron 201 into the 58th Fighter Group created mixed feelings among the US pilots and their ground crews. But before long, the American pilots grew to admire the Aztec Eagles pilots' skills, and they treated the Mexican crews with respect.

The Aztec Eagles took to the sky and commanded their planes with expert maneuvering. By early June, they were flying combat missions as a unit. They targeted enemy concentrations, vehicles, buildings, and weapons. Throughout the month, the pilots carried out ground attacks to support advancing American soldiers on their campaign to liberate Luzon from the Japanese. During this time, the squadron lost two pilots—Lieutenant Fausto Vega Santander and Lieutenant José Espinoza Fuentes— in the line of duty. The loss hit the tightknit group hard.

US general Douglas MacArthur (third from left) welcoming Squadron 201 to Luzon, Philippines

Four Aztec Eagles planes flying in formation

The ground crew kept busy by refueling and rearming the planes and making the frequent repairs the old P-47s required to keep them flying safely. Engines sometimes malfunctioned, and there were many technical problems, but this did not dampen the men's determination to carry out their missions.

In late June, some of the ground crew were assigned to assist in exchanging the squadron's old planes for brand-new P-47s that were waiting for pick-up in New Guinea. The worn-out P-47s were ferried south to Biak, a small island northwest of New Guinea, and exchanged for new replacement planes, which the pilots would fly back to the Philippines.

Ángel Bocanegra was selected to be part of the crew for this ferry mission, and his new duty station was now Biak island.

Ground crew making repairs to old P-47 fighter planes

FERRY MISSIONS, BIAK ISLAND

JULY 14–21, 1945

The Biak assignment to deliver new planes to the Philippines was vital to the performance and safety of the Aztec Eagles. The rest of Squadron 201 had been transferred from Porac to Clark Air Base and were flying more frequent combat missions. They needed the new P-47s as soon as the Biak pilots could ferry them in.

There was no mistaking the new P-47D-30 aircraft. The planes featured a bubble canopy with a 360-degree view. They were painted with red, white, and green Mexican insignia in addition to red, white, and blue United States markings. A white band was painted on the nose. These were the first fighter planes to carry the insignia of both countries.

Ángel was proud to work on Biak and support the ferry mission pilots, who included his friends Captain

Pablo Rivas Martínez, Lieutenant Mario López Portillo, and Lieutenant Héctor Espinosa Galván. The pilots bravely flew over enemy waters on a path made even more difficult by fast-developing typhoons. For the ground crew, each mission meant waiting anxiously and listening for the roar of propellers as the old planes, slated for disposal, neared. Ángel could not relax until the planes touched down and the pilots were safe.

One day as Lieutenant Espinosa Galván prepared for takeoff, Ángel gave his friend a warm smile and saluted as the new P-47D-30 taxied down the runway. And once again Ángel waited and worried.

Lieutenant Espinosa Galván and the other pilots flying that day arrived safely at Clark Air Base. On July 16,

Fighter planes with Mexican tail insignia (left) and United States tail insignia (right) using the same airstrip

the lieutenant set out in an old P-47, headed for Biak. Nearing the island, he got caught in the middle of a wild storm, full of blinding rain and strong winds. Before Lieutenant Espinosa Galván could fly out of the storm, the plane ran out of fuel, crashed, and sank. He did not escape in time.

Three days later, Captain Rivas Martínez hit a sudden thunderstorm as well. Knowing he could run out of fuel, he parachuted out of his plane over the water in an effort to save himself. He was never found.

On July 21, Lieutenant López Portillo took off from Biak. He almost made it to Clark Air Base with the new P-47D-30 when he also flew into a storm. The heavy rain and fog made it impossible to see. Eventually his body and plane were found in a forest on the Bataan Peninsula of Luzon.

The deaths of Lieutenant Espinosa Galván, Captain Rivas Martínez, and Lieutenant López Portillo during their Biak assignment was a major blow for the Aztec Eagles. Ángel's heart ached when he saw the men's personal items gathered up to be returned to their families.

Aztec Eagles pilots lost in battle, from left to right: bottom row: Lieutenant Fausto Vega Santander (eighth in); middle row: Lieutenant Héctor Espinosa Galván (ninth in); top row: Captain Pablo Rivas Martínez (fourth in), Lieutenant José Espinoza Fuentes (fifth in), and Lieutenant Mario López Portillo (sixth in)

COMBAT MISSIONS

JULY–AUGUST 1945

In addition to ferrying new P-47D-30s to Clark Air Base, the Aztec Eagles participated in Very Long Range (VLR) missions over the South China Sea. The pilots flew more than 700 miles (1,126 kilometers) from Manila to Formosa (Taiwan) to strike Japanese targets. The long, dangerous flights were some of the most stressful the pilots had to fly.

The US Navy was preparing to invade Japan, and the Aztec Eagles were assigned to escort a large navy convoy headed north to Japan. The US Navy ships needed to avoid detection. They also needed fighter plane protection from Japanese kamikaze pilots intent on making suicide attacks. The Aztec Eagles flew protective air cover in twelve-hour daylight shifts. At dusk they were relieved of their duties by US night-fighter bombers.

Despite the loss of some pilots, squadron members had to continue combat missions; here they review flight formations

On August 6, the United States dropped an atomic bomb on Hiroshima, Japan; and on August 9, a second bomb was dropped on Nagasaki, Japan. These events brought an end to World War II in Asia.

When the squadron received word on August 26 that the war was over, the men celebrated with shouts of joy. During the three months they were stationed in the Philippines, the Aztec Eagles had completed ninety-six combat missions and nearly two thousand hours of combat flying.

Pilots talking after a VLR combat mission

Aztec Eagles pilots flying in formation near Clark Air Base, Luzon, Phillipines

TRIBUTES TO SQUADRON 201

By all accounts, the Aztec Eagles succeeded in their duty to help the Allied powers defeat the Axis nations. One of the finest tributes to the efforts of Squadron 201 was that there were no deaths attributed to "friendly fire." No Filipino civilians or American military were killed or injured during the squadron's missions.

Before the Aztec Eagles left the Philippines, they were honored for their service and valor in a ceremony on September 16 at Clark Air Base. Philippine commander major general Basilio J. Valdés praised the soldiers as he pinned the Philippine Liberation Medal to their uniforms. Then a single P-47 flew low over the airfield as Squadron 201 stood at attention until the plane disappeared into the clouds.

In Manila, a monument was dedicated on September 25 honoring the five brave men—including the three Biak-mission pilots Lieutenant Espinosa Galván, Captain Rivas Martínez, and Lieutenant López Portillo—who died assisting United States and Filipino troops in the liberation of Luzon. Then on October 23, Air Fighter Squadron 201 left for home on the *Sea Marlin*, a transport ship, headed across the Pacific Ocean for California.

Squadron 201 battle flag, which was returned with honor to Mexican president Ávila Camacho

Squadron mascot Pancho Pistolas (from the film The Three Caballeros) *painted on the tail of a wrecked Japanese bomber at Clark Air Base*

PLAZA DE LA CONSTITUCIÓN, MEXICO CITY, MEXICO

Soldiers of Squadron 201 return to Mexico City and are greeted as heroes

On November 18, 1945, the Aztec Eagles paraded into Mexico City's main plaza. Colonel Antonio Cárdenas Rodríguez, commander of the Mexican Expeditionary Air Force, carried Squadron 201's battle flag and returned it with honor to President Ávila Camacho. The crowd cheered as the president stepped forward, saluted, and accepted the flag.

President Ávila Camacho's voice rose over the cheers of a proud nation gathered in the plaza. "I receive with emotion the flag as a symbol of Mexico. You return with glory, having complied brilliantly with your duty and in these moments, you receive the gratitude of our people," he said.

Tears welled in Ángel's eyes as he stood in parade formation and listened to the president's words. Ángel was proud of his contribution to the war effort, but saddened as he remembered his friends who had not made it home.

When the ceremony ended, Ángel turned and ran into his family's outstretched arms.

Sergeant Ángel Bocanegra, receiving a medal, was recognized for his contributions to World War II, along with the other squadron members

TEPOZTLÁN, MORELOS, MEXICO

NOVEMBER 25, 1945

The dedication ceremony of Tepoztlán's new elementary school was held on November 25. Ángel sat with the members of Squadron 201, who were waiting to hear the president's remarks.

President Ávila Camacho told the crowd that the school had been built with national funds, and by his direct order, because of a promise he had made more than a year earlier to a young sergeant named Ángel Bocanegra del Castillo.

Ángel looked up at the school. "Escuela Escuadrón 201"—Squadron 201 School—was carved above the arches leading into the building where he would soon be teaching. His village now had a school big enough to fit all its students. They would no longer have to sit outside in the brutally hot sun or have classes canceled because of rain.

The crowd burst into applause and rose in standing ovation for the Aztec Eagles, who had fought courageously in the war, and especially for Ángel Bocanegra, who had given their village a school.

Squadron 201 members in front of the completed Escuela Escuadron 201 (Squadron 201 School) in 1945

Students in front of Escuela Escuadron 201 in 2006; the school still welcomes new students every year

A LASTING LEGACY

On December 1, 1945, the Mexican Expeditionary Air Force (FAEM) was disbanded, but its flight operations unit, Air Fighter Squadron 201, is still an active unit in the Mexican Air Force. Squadron 201 remains the only Mexican military force to see overseas combat.

The FAEM's participation in World War II has had a long-lasting impact. The successful wartime partnership between Mexico and the United States fostered an understanding between the people of Mexico and the United States and led to improved relations between the two countries at that time.

Today Squadron 201's battle flag rests in a place of honor in Mexico City's Museo Nacional de Historia—

Monument honoring Squadron 201 in McAllen, Texas

National Museum of History—and an imposing monument to the Aztec Eagles stands in Chapultepec Park. At Mexico's Santa Lucia Air Force Base, a white-nosed P-47D-30 aircraft, bright with Mexican and United States insignia, is on display.

The newest tributes to Squadron 201 are in the United States. A monument was erected at the Veteran's War Memorial of Texas located in McAllen, Texas. On February 26, 2010, the National Museum of the US Air Force revealed a new exhibit dedicated to Mexico's Escuadrón 201. In 2012, US Air Force veteran Alfred Lugo announced plans for a monument in Los Angeles, California, so people of all backgrounds could learn about the Aztec Eagles and their place in Mexican and United States history.

Exhibit dedicated to Squadron 201 at National Museum of the US Air Force

AUTHOR'S NOTE

Perhaps one of the most enduring monuments to Squadron 201 is "the school the Aztec Eagles built." The school still commands the center and heart of the village of Tepoztlán. More than six hundred uniformed children enter the building each day to study.

On a visit to Escuela Escuadrón 201 in March 2006, I met with teachers who had been students of Ángel Bocanegra del Castillo. They were proud to teach in the very classrooms where Maestro Bocanegra had also once taught. They said his presence could still be felt in the hallways and classrooms of the school.

I also met with the fifth and sixth graders in the school library that day. After the students assembled, I made a special request to Señora Conde, the school principal at the time. "Would the students sing for me?" I asked. "Would they sing their school song, the one written by Ángel Bocanegra, 'The Hymn of Squadron 201,' *por favor*?"

A portable keyboard was quickly produced, and a teacher sounded the opening chord. The students' high-pitched voices sang the story of how, almost seventy years earlier, Mexicans and Americans had overcome a troubled history, become allies, and fought alongside one another in World War II.

This book is a further tribute to all those great men and women.

Ángel Bocanegra sitting at a desk in his own classroom

Author Dorinda Makanaōnalani Nicholson (left) meeting Ángel Bocanegra's wife, Laura (center), and daughter, Adela (right)

GLOSSARY AND PRONUNCIATION GUIDE

abolishment (uh-BOL-ish-muhnt): to put an official end to something; to do away with something

Águilas Aztecas (AH-gui-las as-TEH-kas): Aztec Eagles; nickname for Escuadrón Aéreo de Pelea 201 (Air Fighter Squadron 201)

Allied powers (AL-ide POU-urz): alliance of nations (United States, Great Britain, France, Soviet Union, Australia, Belgium, Brazil, Canada, China, Denmark, Greece, Netherlands, New Zealand, Norway, Poland, South Africa, Yugoslavia) that opposed the Axis Powers (Germany, Italy, Japan, Hungary, Romania, Bulgaria) in World War II

ally (AL-eye): person, group, or country that gives aid and/or support to another

Ángel Bocanegra del Castillo (AN-hel boh-kah-NEH-grah del kas-TEEH-yoh): schoolteacher in Tepoztlán, Morelos, Mexico; joined the Mexican army and later, as a sergeant, became a ground crew member of Escuadrón Aéreo de Pelea 201 (Aztec Eagles)

annex (an-EKS *or* AN-eks): to take control of a region or country, often by force

Antonio Cárdenas Rodríguez (an-TOH-nyo KAR-deh-nas ro-DREE-gues): colonel who commanded the Fuerza Aérea Expedicionaria Mexicana (Mexican Expeditionary Air Force)

Antonio López de Santa Anna (an-TOH-nyo LOH-pes de SAN-tah AH-nah): president of Mexico numerous times between 1833 and 1855

atomic bomb (uh-TOM-ik bom): powerful bomb that explodes with great force, heat, and bright light; the explosion results from the energy that is released by splitting atoms

Axis powers (AK-siss POU-urz): alliance of nations (Germany, Italy, Japan, Hungary, Romania, Bulgaria) that opposed the Allied powers (United States, Great Britain, France, Soviet Union, Australia, Belgium, Brazil, Canada, China, Denmark, Greece, Netherlands, New Zealand, Norway, Poland, South Africa, Yugoslavia) in World War II

Basilio J. Valdés (bah-SEE-lyo HOH-tah bal-DES): major general who was commanding officer of the Commonwealth Army and Chief of Staff of the Armed Forces of the Philippines during World War II

Bataan Peninsula (buh-TAN puh-NIN-suh-luh): extension of land located on the western side of Luzon island, Philippines

Biak (bee-YAHK): small island located northwest of New Guinea

bracero (brah-SE-raw): Mexican laborer who worked legally in the United States for a short period of time

Bracero Program (brah-SE-raw PROH-gram): series of laws and agreements between the United States and Mexico that allowed temporary laborers from Mexico to work legally in the US, mostly on farms and railroads

Chapultepec Park (chah-pool-te-PEK park): Mexico City's largest park, covering more than 1,600 acres (645 hectares); known as **Bosque de Chapultepec** (BOHS-keh deh chah-pool-te-PEK) in Spanish

Clark Air Base (klahrk air bayss): former United States Air Force base on Luzon island, Philippines; used during World War II to train pilots from several other countries including Mexico and Brazil

convoy (KON-voi): group of ships and/or vehicles that travel together for convenience or protection

Douglas MacArthur (DUHG-luhs muh-KAHR-ther): general in the United States Army and supreme Allied commander of the Southwest Pacific during World War II

Escuadrón Aéreo de Pelea 201 (es-koo-ah-DRON ah-EH-reh-oh de peh-LEH-ah too-oh-wuhn): Air Fighter Squadron 201

Escuela Escuadrón 201 (es-koo-EH-la es-koo-ah-DRON): Squadron 201 School; built in Tepoztlán, Morelos, Mexico, during World War II and still operating today

Fausto Vega Santander (FAH-oos-toh BEH-gah san-tan-DER): lieutenant who served as a pilot in Escuadrón Aéreo de Pelea 201 (Aztec Eagles)

58th Fighter Group (FIF-tee-eyth FITE-er groop): United States flying unit that operated primarily in the Southwest Pacific Theater as part of the Fifth Air Force

Filipino (fil-uh-PEE-noh): person who was born in or lives in the Philippines

Formosa (for-MOH-suh): island country located off the southeast coast of China; today known as **Taiwan** (tahy-WAHN)

Franklin D. Roosevelt (FRANGK-lin dee ROH-zuh-velt): president of the United States from 1933 to 1945

friendly fire (FREND-lee fire): weapon fire by one's own forces, especially when it harms one's own troops

Fuerza Aérea Expedicionaria Mexicana (foo-UR-sah ah-EH-reh-ah eks-peh-deeh-see-oh-NAH-ryah meh-hee-KAH-nah): abbreviated as FAEM; Mexican Expeditionary Air Force

Golden Gate Bridge (GOHL-duhn geyt brij): bridge connecting northern California with San Francisco peninsula

Good Neighbor policy (gud NAY-bur POL-uh-see): United States foreign policy doctrine, adopted by President Franklin D. Roosevelt in 1933, designed to improve relations with the nations of Central and South America

Héctor Espinosa Galván (EK-tor es-pee-NOH-sah gal-BAN): lieutenant who served as a pilot in Escuadrón Aéreo de Pelea 201 (Aztec Eagles)

Hiroshima (heer-oh-SHEE-muh *or* heh-ROH-she-muh): city in Japan; site of first atomic bomb explosion (August 6, 1945) during World War II

insignia (in-SIG-nee-uh): badge, emblem, or sign that shows a person's rank or membership in an organization; a special mark or sign

José Espinoza Fuentes (ho-SE es-pee-NOH-sah foo-EN-tes): lieutenant who served as a pilot in Escuadrón Aéreo de Pelea 201 (Aztec Eagles)

kamikaze (kah-mi-KAH-zee): member of a group of Japanese pilots in World War II trained to crash their planes into enemy targets, especially ships

Laura Quiroz Concha (LAH-ooh-rah kee-ROS KON-ya): schoolteacher in Tepoztlán, Morelos, Mexico; wife of Ángel Bocanegra del Castillo

Luzon (loo-ZON): largest island of the Philippines; located in the northern part of the country

maestro (MAHY-stroh): master or teacher

Majors Field (MAY-jurs feeld): former airfield in Greenville, Texas, established for training pilots and crew of United States Army Air Force fighter planes, especially P-47 Thunderbolts

Manila (muh-NIL-uh): capital of the Philippines, located on Luzon island

Manuel Ávila Camacho (mah-noo-EL AH-bee-lah ka-MAH-yoh): president of Mexico from 1940 to 1946

Mario López Portillo (MAH-ryoh LOH-pes pohr-TEE-yoh): lieutenant who served as a pilot in Escuadrón Aéreo de Pelea 201 (Aztec Eagles)

mi presidente (mee preh-see-DEN-teh): my president

Morelos (maw-RE-laws): one of the states of Mexico; located in the south-central part of the country

Museo Nacional de Historia (moo-SEH-oh nah-see-oh-NAHL de ees-TOH-ryah): National Museum of History; museum in Mexico City that contains objects related to Mexican history

Nagasaki (nah-guh-SAH-kee): city in Japan; site of second atomic bomb explosion (August 9, 1945) during World War II

Neftalí González Corona (neph-tah-LEE gohn-SAH-les koh-ROH-nah): sergeant who served as a pilot in Escuadrón Aéreo de Pelea 201 (Aztec Eagles)

New Guinea (nyoo GIN-ee): large island located in the southwest Pacific Ocean

P-47 Thunderbolt (pee-for-TEE-sev-UHN THUHN-der-bohlt): rugged, powerful fighter plane used by United States Army Air Force during World War II; later replaced by the P-47D-30 Thunderbolt

Pablo Rivas Martínez (PAH-bloh REE-bas mahr-TEE-nes): captain who served as a pilot in Escuadrón Aéreo de Pelea 201 (Aztec Eagles)

Peh-Cuas (peh-COO-ahs): Aztec Eagles' Spanish nickname for P-47 Thunderbolts

Philippines (FIL-uh-peenz *or* fil-uh-PEENZ): country made up of thousands of islands located in the Pacific Ocean southeast of China

Pocatello Air Force Base (poh-kuh-TEL-oh air forss bayss): airfield in Pocatello, Idaho, established for training pilots and crew of United States Army Air Force fighter planes

Porac (poh-RAK): airfield on Luzon island, Philippines

por favor (pohr fa-VOHR): please

Radamés Gaxiola Andrade (rah-dah-MEHS gak-see-OH-lah an-DRAH-deh): captain who was squadron commander of Escuadrón Aéreo de Pelea 201 (Aztec Eagles)

ratify (RAT-uh-fye): to make an agreement, treaty, or law official by signing it or voting for it

reconciliation (rek-uhn-sil-ee-EY-shuhn): to become friendly again after an argument or a disagreement; when former enemies agree to a truce

San Jacinto (sahn hah-SEEN-toh): site of an important battle (April 21, 1836) of the Texas Revolution

solidarity (sol-uh-DA-ruh-tee): unity; agreement among people that they will work or fight together to achieve a common goal

summit (SUHM-it): meeting or series of meetings between important leaders of two or more governments

Tejas (TEH-has): Texas

Tepoztlán (teh-pohs-TLAN): village in the state of Morelos in south-central Mexico

torpedo (tor-PEE-doh): to attack (a ship) from underwater with an explosive, missile-shaped bomb

treaty (TREE-tee): official agreement between two or more nations or groups

typhoon (tye-FOON): violent, destructive tropical storm in the western Pacific Ocean region

U-boat (YOO-bote): German submarine used during World War I and World War II

US-Mexican War (yoo-ess-MEK-si-kuhn wor): armed conflict between the United States and Mexico that lasted from 1846 to 1848

Very Long Range mission (VER-ee lawng reynj MISH-uhn): abbreviated as VLR mission; assignment to fly long distances over the South China Sea to attack enemy targets during World War II

Women's Army Corps (WIM-inz AHR-mee kohr): abbreviated as WAC; women's branch of the United States Army from 1943 until 1978, after which the women's units were integrated into the men's army units

World War II (wurld wor too): war fought mainly in Asia, Europe, and North Africa from 1939 to 1945

AUTHOR'S SOURCES

"Among Them a Modest Citizen of Tepoztlán: 58 years ago, a group of heroes faced the Taste of War." *Tepoztlán* magazine, August 2002.

Bocanegra, Adela. Personal interview with Ángel Bocanegra's daughter, translated by R. E. Roman. Tepoztlán, Mexico, March 13, 2006.

———. Phone interview, translated by Paul Baum. December 20, 2007.

———. Personal interview by Silvia Ballinas. September and October 2012, January and February 2013.

Calvo, Dana. "The Saga of the Aztec Eagles." *Los Angeles Times*, July 25, 2004. http://articles.latimes.com/2004/jul/25/magazine/tm-mexpilots30.

Campos, Magda Hernandez. Personal interview with the vice principal of Escuela Escuadrón 201, translated by R. E. Roman. Tepoztlán, Mexico, March 13, 2006.

Carnes, Bryan D. "Remembering the 'Aztec Eagles.'" National Museum of the US Air Force, March 2, 2010. http://www.nationalmuseum.af.mil/news/story.asp?id=123192836.

Conde, Maria Cedeño. Personal interview with the director of Escuela Escuadrón 201, translated by R. E. Roman. Tepoztlán, Mexico, March 13, 2006.

Crawford, Mark. *Encyclopedia of the Mexican-American War*. Santa Barbara, CA: ABC-CLIO, 1999.

de la Peña, José Enrique. *With Santa Anna in Texas: A Personal Narrative of the Revolution*. Trans. Carmen Perry. College Station: Texas A&M University Press, 1975.

Eisenhower, John S. D. *So Far from God: The U.S. War with Mexico 1846–1848*. New York: Random House, 1989.

Gomez, Yolanda Demesa. Personal interview with a teacher at Escuela Escuadrón 201. Tepoztlán, translated by R. E. Roman. Tepoztlán, Mexico, March 13, 2006.

Guevara, Lucy. "Reynaldo Perez Gallard." The University of Texas at Austin VOCES Oral History Project, 2005. http://www.lib.utexas.edu/voces/template-stories-indiv.html?work_urn=urn%3Autlol%3Awwlatin.037&work_title=Gallardo%2C+Reynaldo+Perez.

Hagedorn, Dan. *Republic P-47 Thunderbolt: The Final Chapter Latin American Air Forces Service*. St. Paul, MN: Phalanx Publishing Co. Ltd., 1992.

Lewis, Oscar. *Tepoztlán: Village in Mexico*. New York: Holt, Rinehart and Winston, 1960.

Morales, Francisco Javier Cortes. Personal interview with a teacher at Escuela Escuadrón 201, translated by R. E. Roman. Tepoztlán, Mexico, March 13, 2006.

Rodriguez, Marrissa. "The Legend of Pancho Pistolas." *Hispanic* 19, no. 11 (November 2006), 32.

Romano, Lt. Col. Susan A. "Remembering the 'Forgotten Eagles.'" CONR-1AF (AFNORTH): US Air Force, November 6, 2009. http://www.1af.acc.af.mil/news/story.asp?id=123176493.

Sandoval Castarrica, Enrique. *Historia oficial de la Fuerza Aérea Expedicionaria Mexicana*. Mexico: Secretaría de la Defensa Nacional, 1946.

Tudor, William G. "Flight of Eagles: the Mexican Expeditionary Air Force Escuadron 201 in World War II." Dissertation. Fort Worth: Texas Christian University, 1997.

Unander Jr., Sig. "Strike of the Aztec Eagles!" Air Art Northwest, 2008. www.airartnw.com/aztec_eagles_story.htm.

"World War II: Mexican Air Force Helped Liberate the Philippines." *Aviation History* magazine, June 12, 2006. http://www.historynet.com/world-war-ii-mexican-air-force-helped-liberate-the-philippines.htm.

QUOTATION SOURCES

page 8: "I repeat to . . . devotion to liberty." Quoted from "Good Neighbors—Good Friends: Mexico the Bridge Between Latin and Saxon Cultures." Speech by Manuel Ávila Camacho, President of the Republic of Mexico, April 20, 1943. http://www.ibiblio.org/pha/policy/1943/1943-04-20b.html.

page 10: "I am Ángel . . . of Tepoztlán, Morelos." Quoted during personal interview with the family of Ángel Bocanegra. Tepoztlán, Mexico, March 13, 2006.

page 20: "The journey was . . . of the squadron." Quoted in "World War II: Mexican Air Force Helped Liberate the Philippines." *Aviation History* magazine, June 12, 2006. http://www.historynet.com/world-war-ii-mexican-air-force-helped-liberate-the-philippines.htm.

page 29: "I receive with . . . of our people." Quoted in "Remembering the 'Forgotten Eagles'" by Lt. Col. Susan A. Romano. CONR-1AF (AFNORTH): US Air Force, November 6, 2009. http://www.1af.acc.af.mil/news/story.asp?id=123176493.

ACKNOWLEDGMENTS

The author thanks these generous people for their help to make this book possible: Adela Bocanegra, Felix Vargas Navarette and family; Señora Conde, former principal of Escuela Escuadron 201; maestro Morales; maestra Yolanda Gomez.; translators R. E. Roman, Silvia Ballinas Tapia, Paul Baum, Nick and Martha Gomez; Helen McDonald and Rich Koone, National Museum of the Pacific War; consultants Sig Unander and Victor Mancilla; researcher Mario Longoria, Southwest Historical Studies; Terrill Aitken, Senior Curator, National Museum of the United States Air Force; Dr. Pedro Loureiro, Archivist/Historian, Defense Imagery Management Operations Center–Records; Billy Wade, Senior Archivist, Still Picture Branch, National Archives; Dr. Trinidad Gonzales, Department of History and Philosophy, South Texas College; Alberto González Ramírez; and everyone from the Asociación Mexicana de Veteranos de la II Guerra Mundial.

Photograph Credits

Smithsonian National Air and Space Museum: front cover, pp. 17 (NASM 86-5570), 23 (top, NASM 86-5568), 24 (NASM 86-5567), 27 (bottom right, NASM 86-5569); National Archives: back cover (photo no. 342_FH-3A-30471-57828AC), pp. 14 (left, photo no. 44-PA-254), 17 (inset, photo no. 111-SC-212422), 22 (bottom left, photo no. 111-SC-207980) and (top right, photo no. 111-SC-352183), 23 (bottom right, NASM 342-FH3A-30669-60767AC); Archivo del Museo Militar de Aviación de la Fuerza Aérea Mexicana: pp. 2–3, 10–11, 12 (bottom left), 13, 14 (bottom right), 15, 19, 20–21, 25, 26, 27 (top right), 28 (left), 29, 30; public domain: p. 12 (top right); map courtesy of Rethinking Schools: p. 4; Benson Latin American Collection, University of Texas at Austin: p. 5 (top left); University of North Texas Libraries: p. 5 (bottom right); courtesy of Ángel Bocanegra's family: pp. 6, 29, 33; Historical Society of Palm Beach County (HSPBC): p. 7; Franklin D. Roosevelt Presidential Library & Museum: p. 8; Leonard Nadel Photographs and Scrapbooks, Archives Center, National Museum of American History, Smithsonian Institution: p. 9; Russell Lee Photograph Collection, e_rl_14646_0038, The Dolph Briscoe Center for American History, University of Texas at Austin: p. 16; US Air Force: p. 28 (right); courtesy of Larry Nicholson: pp. 31, 33 (bottom right); National Museum of the US Air Force: p. 32 (bottom left); Veteran's War Memorial of Texas, McAllen, Texas: p. 32 (top right).

Text copyright © 2016 by Dorinda Makanaōnalani Nicholson
LEE & LOW BOOKS Inc., 95 Madison Avenue, New York, NY 10016, leeandlow.com
Book design by David and Susan Neuhaus/NeuStudio
Book production by The Kids at Our House
The text is set in 12.5 Myriad Pro
Manufactured in China by Imago, July 2016
Printed on paper from responsible sources

10 9 8 7 6 5 4 3 2 1
First Edition

Library of Congress Cataloging-in-Publication Data
Nicholson, Dorinda Makanaonalani Stagner.
The school the Aztec Eagles built / by Dorinda Makanaonalani Nicholson. — First edition.
pages cm
Summary: "A photo-illustrated book about the Aztec Eagles, Mexico's World War II Air Force squadron interwoven with the story of Sergeant Angel Bocanegra, whose service was rewarded with the building of a school in his village. Includes glossary, author's note, and author's sources"—Provided by publisher.
Audience: K to grade 3.
Includes bibliographical references.
ISBN 978-1-60060-440-9 (hardcover : alkaline paper)
1. Mexico. Fuerza Aérea Expedicionaria Mexicana. Escuadrón Aérea de Pelea 201—History—Juvenile literature. 2. World War, 1939-1945—Aerial operations, Mexican—Juvenile literature. 3. World War, 1939–1945—Aerial operations, American—Juvenile literature. 4. World War, 1939-1945—Campaigns—Philippines—Luzon—Juvenile literature. 5. Bocanegra, Angel, 1918—Juvenile literature. 6. Bocanegra, Angel, 1918—Awards—Juvenile literature. 7. Airmen—Mexico—Biography—Juvenile literature. 8. Teachers—Mexico—Tepoztlán—Biography—Juvenile literature. 9. School buildings—Mexico—Tepoztlán—Design and construction—History—20th century—Juvenile literature. 10. Tepoztlán (Mexico)—History—20th century—Juvenile literature. I. Title.
D792.M6N42 2015   940.54'4972—dc23   2014047757